THE

VOICE OVER STARTUP GUIDE

HOW TO LAND YOUR FIRST VO JOB

CHRIS AGOS

www.complete-voiceover.com

Voice Over and Voice Acting Series:

The Voice Over Startup Guide: How To Land Your First VO Job

Published by **www.complete-voiceover.com**

ISBN: 978-0-9828863-6-6

Cover Image Copyright: Shutterstock – PrinceOfLove

CONTENTS

ABOUT CHRIS AGOS

Chris Agos launched his acting and voice over career in 1995. As a voice talent, Chris quickly developed a reputation for efficiency and professionalism on the job, resulting in a career spanning thousands of projects from commercials to corporate to narration and beyond.

As an on-camera actor, he appears in TV shows across various networks and streaming services. Chris has taught voice acting since 2007 and has authored a number of books on the subject, helping voice actors aim for the highest levels of the industry by taking a big-picture view of each project and magnifying it with storytelling.

He continues to audition, work, and help others get what they want from their voice over and acting careers. A Chicago native, he lives in Los Angeles with his wife and twin sons.

https://www.instagram.com/chrisagos/

https://twitter.com/chrisagos

https://www.youtube.com/chrisagosactor

https://www.imdb.me/chrisagos

https://www.chrisagos.com

https://www.complete-voiceover.com

https://www.actinginchicago.com

Visit **www.complete-voiceover.com** for free coaching videos and more books on voice over and voice acting.

INTRODUCTION

I've been teaching and writing about voice over (VO) for over a decade, and if there's one thing I've learned, it's that people from all walks of life are interested in it. I've taught dentists and judges, chefs and brick layers, college students, insurance adjusters, and stay-at-home moms. All of them started just like I did: with little to no knowledge about the voice over industry.

It's not exactly easy to get a comprehensive look at the world of voice over (or voice acting; the terms are interchangeable). It is just so vast. It can be overwhelming to know where to begin.

That's precisely why I wrote this book. Learning anything new is challenging, but it can be especially tough if you're getting small bits of information from multiple sources. Hopping online is how most people learn about something that interests them. They get glimpses of the story from general search results, topical forums, and videos.

But that's a bad way to learn about voice acting because there's so much variation in the business. Cobbling together knowledge from a dozen sources (some of them more reliable than others) can lead to more confusion than understanding.

Maybe you've experienced this yourself. Have you watched videos on home recording? Read comment threads on the pros and cons of working with a talent agent? If you have, you're likely more confused than when you started.

I'd like to congratulate you on taking the first step toward getting a well-organized bird's-eye view of how to get started in the industry. Yes, you can spend endless hours online finding all this stuff, but I prefer a methodical, efficient approach to learning. It's not only my own personal preference but that of the industry. As your knowledge of the business grows, you'll discover that it rewards efficiency. Might as well get used to that now.

Because so much goes into starting a career in voice acting, my goal is to distill all the information you'll need down to just the relevant bits. I'll slow down all the moving parts, so you can get a good look at the machine. This will allow you to decide where you might focus your effort. I'll even teach you a couple of my secret moves, so you can grease the machine and make it work more smoothly for you.

The business wasn't always as complicated as it is today. When I started my career twenty years ago, the voice over industry wasn't even an industry. It was more like a supply closet down the hall from the marketing department of the fourth-largest company in an industry. It was a well-hidden secret.

I don't know exactly why you bought this book, but I'm willing to guess that at least one of these things is true: You've been told you have a great voice. You've heard that voice actors make good money working at home. Or you're an actor who knows there's a whole world of work available to you, but you don't know where to start. Or maybe you're just curious.

Here's how I got into the business.

I grew up wanting to be a doctor, so that was my track in college. Applying to medical school meant taking a standardized exam covering all manner of math and science. I needed a distraction, one totally unrelated to medicine.

One day I picked up a copy of the campus newspaper and saw an ad that spoke to me. No, it screamed at me. This was before the internet, so the only way I could find out more was to call the phone number.

I did.

I got nervous.

I hung up.

Eventually I called back, and because of that phone call, I never went to medical school.

The ad was for private voice over lessons. I knew there were people who made a living with their voice, and I was always curious about how they did it. Here was a chance to meet one of them, and try something new.

I could have passed on the chance to sign up. I had plenty of other things keeping me busy, and this seemed pretty far from anything I was doing in school. But something told me to give it a go.

I was terrible. But I was also hooked. It's entirely possible you will also be terrible when you start, but maybe you'll be hooked too.

Signing up for coaching was a risk, but it really paid off. I continued practicing and eventually started to get some paying work. More than twenty years later, I've been the voice of some of the biggest brands around, helped countless people learn new things, and even branched into on-camera acting. I've walked red carpets in Hollywood, guest-starred on some of my favorite TV shows, and played iconic historical figures.

All thanks to voice over. I can't imagine doing anything else for a living.

I wish I could tell you that great voice of yours is all you need to make this work, but that's just not true. In today's industry, your performance ability is much more important than the quality of your voice. The good news is that how well you read is entirely within your control. In a business where many things are out of your control, you need to focus on the things that are. Your vocal quality is not. You have what you have.

If you've been told dump trucks filled with cash pull up to the back doors of voice talent's homes on a daily basis, boy, are you going to be disappointed. They pull up to the front door.

Kidding, of course. Don't get me wrong, there are people making seven figures a year in this business, but they're the exception, not the rule. It is very possible your annual income could approach six figures. I wouldn't say everyone is earning that much, but it's much more common than those seven-figure people. It all depends on your work ethic and which corners of the business you focus on.

You don't need to have a cool voice, and you may not earn enough to buy a minor league baseball team, but if you're an actor, you might feel very comfortable behind a microphone. Voice over is acting, just without the help of nonverbal communication. That's a tough thing for some actors to get into their heads, but it's learnable, and your acting background will give you a head start.

Thankfully, you don't have to be an actor to be a fantastic voice talent. If you're simply curious about the business, you're in the right place. I'm happy to share my experience because I've had some huge wins and made more than my fair share of mistakes. I've voiced almost everything there is to voice, encountered every kind of director, and read some of the greatest and the worst copy in the world.

In the coming pages you'll learn about reading, recording, and repetition. I'll explain agents, training, and marketing. You'll learn how to manage expectations and apply good business sense to your new venture.

We'll cover a good amount of detail, but this is a guide for beginners who need a lot of start-up information in one place. If you want to dive deeper, visit Complete-Voiceover.com and subscribe to my YouTube channel. Those resources are growing all the time.

I wrote this book with two goals in mind. First, to show you an accurate, big-picture view of the voice over industry as it stands today. You can only make good decisions in the context of the business as a whole.

I also aim to give you an actionable plan for launching a career. I'll spell out seven steps which, if you follow them, will put you on a path to having a VO career no matter where you live or how much time you can devote to it. This will allow you to set realistic goals and avoid making some of the mistakes I made.

Why seven? It's a reasonable number. If I gave you forty steps, you'd say, "That's too much work, I don't want to do this." If I gave you three steps, you'd say, "Does this guy think I'm stupid? No one can start a career in three steps." So I broke it down into seven. Here they are:

1. Listen

2. Train

3. Find Your Focus

4. Invest in Gear

5. Build Demos

6. Market

7. Repeat

Let's get busy.

GET THE AUDIO

We've put together a collection of audio files to go along with examples in this book. They're available to download for free at Complete-Voiceover.com. The link is at the top of the home page. Reading about voice over is great, but your learning will be much more complete if you also hear examples of voice over work.

We recommend first saving the files to your computer. From there you can add them to your media library and transfer them to your tablet, phone, or any other device. They are mp3 files, so you can import them into a sound editor or even burn them to a CD. If you need technical support, please email us via the site's contact form.

Kindle/eReaders

To get the most out of this book, turn off column viewing and hold your Kindle in landscape mode.

Get your audio now for free. You'll learn so much more if you do!

www.complete-voiceover.com

STEP ONE: LISTEN

You might think your voice is the thing you'll use most as a voice over talent, but you'd be wrong. It's your ear.

If you've ever seen footage from a rock concert, you may have noticed band members wearing in-ear monitors on stage. They look like hearing aids. They serve two functions: to protect musicians' hearing and to allow them to hear themselves relative to the rest of the band. Without that feedback, the noise of the concert would make it impossible to hear their own performance, leaving them with no hypothetical target to aim at. They'd have no idea if they were in time, in tune, or not.

Your ear is the key to how you sound because it allows you to monitor yourself and those around you. As a voice actor, you need to be good at listening. Humans primarily rely on their sight to get them through the day, but our hearing is a close second. We just need to refine that sense as it applies to voice over.

There are three points in time when this will be especially important: when you're learning to identify different styles of reading out loud (known as reads), when you're doing your own reads, and when you're being asked to adjust your reads to give your client something they need. If you can't monitor feedback and adjust accordingly at any of those points, this career is going to be a struggle.

Identifying Read Styles

Let's start with commercials. That's my specialty and a subject I like to make videos about, but it's also a basic skill. Every voice talent should be able to analyze ad copy (scripts written by commercial copywriters) and come up with a good commercial read.

Maybe you've never really listened to commercials before. You've heard them, but listening is different. Hearing is like glancing at a painting and noticing it's a landscape. Listening is noticing that it brings you somewhere. Maybe it reminds you of your childhood or a favorite vacation destination. Taking the analogy further, listening critically means leaning in close enough to see the brushstrokes so you understand how the artist created the image and why it made you feel what you felt.

We want to listen for that level of detail in commercials. We're going to look for the brushstrokes in the voice over.

There's a great site called iSpot.tv that archives thousands of commercials, and I like to use it as a research tool. Take thirty minutes, go there, and browse ads. I'll wait.

Close your eyes while you play some commercials (called spots in the ad world) and just listen. After a while you'll notice they don't just sound different; they have moods. Like paintings, they conjure different emotions. Some make you smile; others intrigue you. The combination of what's being said and how the voice actor is saying it adds up to something you can describe. As you listen, try to pick out attitudes the talent adopts as they're reading.

Friendly. Aspirational. Confident. Secretive. Tempting. Knowledgeable. Excited.

Need a few examples? Sure thing. Below is a collection of commercial copy with a description of the read style that made it to air. All of them are rewritten versions of actual commercials. As much as I would like to use the original scripts and audio from those spots, copyrights and trademarks prevent me from doing so. Instead, I've modified the copy and replaced every brand name with a generic one: "Harry's." You'll see that Harry's sells everything from skin care to SUVs.

If you haven't already, now's the time to visit Complete-Voiceover.com to get the free audio files associated with all the examples in this book. You'll be able to listen to a performance of each script. Combining reading with listening will be the best and fastest way to learn.

Here's a friendly read.

Example 1a

> Here's to making your mornings just a little better.
>
> The sweet, savory, egg and cheese croissant sandwich.
>
> Breakfast. At Harry's.

This guy is friendly and knowledgeable.

Example 1b

> Jason knows how to keep his wheels spinning.
>
> That's why he starts his day with those famous scoops.
>
> And delicious, heart healthy oat meal.
>
> By taking steps to lead a healthy lifestyle,
>
> Jason knows he'll be ready for life's curveballs.
>
> Harry's oatmeal. And try oatmeal crunch with nutty oat clusters.

Take a listen to someone who is folksy and trustworthy.

Example 1c

> We know the value of trust. We built our business on it.
>
> Back when the country went west for gold, we were the ones who carried it back east.
>
> Over the years, we built on that trust. We always made that effort.
>
> Today we still operate the same way. Trust. In your hands.

Here's a guy who's compassionate.

Example 1d

> Mike woke up with a sore knee. But he's got work to do. He can't afford to miss today's deadlines.
>
> He relies on Harry's to get past the pain, and get him through the day.
>
> If he'd taken anything else, he be taking more pills right now.
>
> Only Harry's has the strength to stop tough pain all day long.
>
> No other pain reliever can do that.
>
> Harry's. Relief, all day long.

And here's a read with quiet confidence.

Example 1e

> At Harry's, we turn emotions into jewelry. Jewelry that tells her you never want to let her go.
>
> In a way that's so much more than words.

It could be a piece our designers created for our exclusive collections.

Or it could be something made just for her.

The one gift that tells her exactly how you feel about her. That's Harry's.

This talent is simply wowed by everything she's saying.

Example 1f

Do you dread shopping for jeans? Are you fed up with jeans that just don't fit?
Introducing Harry's Jeans. The super cute, one size fits always denim.
It's a customized, perfect fit for every woman, every shape, every time.
No matter the size, Harry's Jeans will always fit you perfectly!

This read has a little wink of shared knowledge to it.

Example 1g

Blind dates can feel uncomfortable enough. Your clothes shouldn't add to the problem.

Harry's. The most comfortable.

Here's a tough-guy read, which is pretty common for trucks.

Example 1h

Bigger doesn't mean stronger.

Think capability, not weight class.

Introducing the Harry, the all new compact SUV.

Mighty. Without being massive.

The all new Harry. In showrooms now.

This girl sounds like the girl next door who's happy she gets to share some news.

Example 1i

You are many different things in one amazing package.

And Harry's lets you express every one.

No one brings you more must-have brands and must have prices.

You can shop online, or take it home today.

You can always save on something for every you.

Harry's.

And this is a straight announce read, just telling it like it is.

Example 1j

Nails lose moisture over time.

Harry's Total Hydration Moisture Plus.

Our 100% natural moisturizing formula hydrates and strengthens your nails.

For nails that won't go unnoticed.

This is what's called a retail read, where it's all about the deal.

Example 1k

> Don't miss out. It's the final days of Harry's Year End Sales Event.
>
> Hurry in for big savings. On all the names you know and love.
>
> Like the most capable and sporty SUV in its class.
>
> Now available for $199/month for 36 months
>
> But all good things must come to an end. So hurry in.

Listen to this campy, retro read.

Example 1l

> We've supported American heroes for decades. Patton. Ruth. Armstrong, who went to the moon.
>
> But imagine if Neil had worn today's Harry's Underwear.
>
> He would have planted the flag on every moon.
>
> Giving America dibs on the entire galaxy.
>
> Harry's Underwear. Supporting American heroes big and small for decades.

This woman sounds like she knows way more than you do.

Example 1m

> Harry's Paris presents new Color Match Glisten.
>
> Our first lipstick with microfine oils and one hundred percent natural pigments that match and enhance your own lip color.
>
> For glossy application and maximum impact.
>
> New Color Match Glisten. From Harry's Paris. Glisten it up.

This talent sounds really calm but is speaking quickly at the same time. Tricky to pull off.

Example 1n

New Sheer Complete, by Harry's Minerals.

Our first ever tone-correcting sealing foundation.

One silky drop means luminous, even, flawless silky skin.

No parabens, oils, animal products, or fragrance.

Sheer Complete, by Harry's Minerals.

And this guy is a great storyteller.

Example 1o

This is the story of springtime's biggest fan.

April was born on the first day of spring, and from an early age, she loved that time of year.

New flowers and rain showers, cute dresses, and bands for her tresses.

Which brings us to the very moment she fell for springtime all over again.

Was she expecting to find the perfect designer boots at such an amazing price?

No. But that's the thing about a store full of surprises.

April never knows what she's going to find at Harry's. But she knows she's going to love it.

By now you realize there are a million different ways to interpret ad copy, but they're all useless if you can't tell the difference between them. If you're asked to sound like you're sharing a secret with a friend but you instead do a straight announce read, you will not get that job. When you train your brain to listen critically, you'll be able to describe reads in terms of how they make you feel, identify the attitude the talent was trying to convey when they spoke, and apply that to your own reads.

Once you're really paying attention, you'll recognize shifts within reads. Sometimes attitudes change from one moment to the next. Let me show you what I mean.

Wells Fargo Bank recently aired a commercial that got a lot of attention. The entire spot is driven by the VO, and it's amazingly well done. It's so good that I made a video about it on my YouTube channel, where I break down the read line by line.

The copy begins by describing the company's history. There's a quiet pride in the talent's voice as he moves through the years. Then, twenty-two seconds into the spot, he sounds ever so mildly taken by surprise when he says the company lost their way. And as he continues to tell the story, he is ever more hopeful, quietly excited to share all the changes the company is committed to making. The read crescendos, like a concerto, until he's halfway begging us to believe him when he says, "Because earning back your trust is our greatest priority." Then he backs off, and lands the spot barely impressed with the notion of rebirth. He just tells it like it is: "Established 1852. Re-established 2018." The subtext? You trusted us back then, and you can still trust us today.

He never gets much above a whisper. He doesn't need to add volume; he makes his point through pacing, inflections, pauses, and rhythm. He doesn't over enunciate or change his personality. He is the same guy through it all and makes microadjustments to push all those emotional buttons. Bravo to all involved.

Does it surprise you there's this amount of detail in commercial reads? It shouldn't. Hundreds of thousands of dollars are spent on commercials. Advertisers and their ad agencies want a return on their investment. Their message has to be 100 percent clear, no matter if the client spent ten thousand or ten million dollars, and the talent's read can be a huge part of the success or failure of that message.

Because a lot is riding on the success of any voice over job, decision makers put a lot of trust in their voice talent. It's a big responsibility, so I can't overstate the importance of knowing how to build reads that make sense for the job on which you've been hired.

Your Reads

I chose commercials as a starting point because it's so easy to find examples of good work, but there are a couple exercises that'll help you develop a feel for reading in any category: promos, audiobook narration, e-learning, etc.

Because voice over is mostly a solitary business, voice actors self-direct. When you're new to the business, you can jump-start your training by finding inspiration in the reads that are already out there.

So give this a try: choose a script from the previous pages, and read it with several different attitudes or intentions. Start with friendly and knowledgeable, then move on to happy and excited, then be absolutely wowed by what you're saying, then read it with the voice of authority. Always try to tell a story with the copy. That idea, of being a storyteller first and foremost, will carry you far in this business and keep your career rolling.

Not every style is going to make sense for every script, but that's not the point. The goal is to feel what it's like to deliver a script in one attitude versus another. That's a huge part of what voice talent do on a daily basis in auditions and sessions.

Speaking of auditions, know that you'll always have to audition to get work. Even as you progress through your career, you'll still have to read for just about every new job you get. Bill Lloyd, one of the busiest promo voices in Los Angeles and author of the forthcoming *Voice Over and Voice Acting: Mastering Promos*, had a coach who went further than that.

"In my very first session with him, he told me that auditioning is the job. If you get invited back to actually record, fine. That's gravy. But auditioning is the job."

There will be clients who hire you without one, but the only people who sometimes don't have to audition are celebrities, and even they have to audition sometimes. Since you and I aren't celebs (I've been on TV, but that hardly admits me into the rarefied world of direct booking), we'll do the majority of our auditions at home with no one to give feedback. That means you need a guide to follow, which you can build yourself.

As you go down the iSpot rabbit hole, take copious notes. Develop a list of read styles and attitudes along with links to corresponding examples. Need a reference for a friendly read? I'd find any spot from a cereal brand. If I wanted to know what someone means by a retail read, I'd reference a car ad. Maybe your list looks something like this:

ATTITUDE	LINK	NOTES
Friendly	https://www.ispot.tv/ad/ARBX/kelloggs-raisin-bran-father-and-daughter-bike-a-thon-crunch	I'd want this guy as a neighbor, seems like a nice person.
Retail	https://www.ispot.tv/ad/w0Ju/nissan-now-sales-event-cant-miss-still-time-to-save	A little excitement, but not too much. Makes me feel like I might miss something if I don't act on it.
Good Storytelling	https://www.ispot.tv/ad/ACyC/ marshalls-falls-biggest-fan	I want to know more about what he's talking about. Makes me smile.

If you do enough research, you'll eventually have examples of just about everything that will come up in audition specs, character descriptions that almost always accompany the audition script. These might consist of a couple words or several paragraphs detailing the kind of voice the client is looking for. Specs are sometimes very helpful, sometimes cryptic, and sometimes useless. Here are some real life examples taken from recent auditions:

Client: Cable TV Provider
Male, 30–40, conversational, trustworthy, authentic and approachable, not salesy.

Client: General Retailer
Female, 20s–30s, youthful and intelligent. Open ethnicity. Knows something we don't and can't wait to tell us without being too excited or pushy.

Client: Pharmaceuticals
30–50, mom, an everyday neighbor. Overwhelmed by pain but in control, someone who can communicate minor pain issues without coming off as sad or complaining.

Client: Automaker
Truck guy, not too old, a little gravel but not too much, chops wood for fun, announces without being announcery.

Client: Bank
30–40, natural read, think storyteller versus announcer. Expressive but not overly serious/dramatic.

You can see that some of these specs are pretty specific, while others just give us a general feel for what the client might want to hear. The pharma casting contains a contradiction. The character is overwhelmed by pain but has "minor" pain issues. The truck guy has to announce without being "announcery."

Very often, the decision makers will know what they want only when they hear it, so we have to come as close as we can to what they say they're looking for.

Your reference reads can help you enormously. When you get a script and the specs, use them as a starting point. Then build your performance around those attitudes and listen to other spots for inspiration. There's no shame in copying what worked for another voice talent. We all learn from each other.

Adjusting Reads

The ability to adjust reads is perhaps the most valuable skill a voice actor can have. Our first take is almost never what winds up being in the final spot, and the journey to the last take can be productive and fruitful for our client or woefully frustrating. Our job is to make it a positive experience, and we do that by adjusting our reads to their needs.

The worst thing you can do is get locked into one way of saying things. That shows you're worrying about how you're saying the copy instead of what story you're trying to tell. You don't know who you're talking to or why you're saying what you're saying. Instead, you're reading. We'll talk more about this in the next chapter, but just know that being adaptable is a highly valued skill.

There are many reasons why you might be asked to make adjustments. You may have to adjust for time (slower or faster), hit this word or downplay that one, bring more smile to the read, talk to one person instead of another, adopt a certain attitude for one sentence and switch to a different one for the next, and on and on.

Your listening skills will come in very handy, only this time you're not necessarily listening to reads, you're listening to a producer or client's direction. Sometimes those people know exactly how to get what they need from you. Often, they don't know how to talk to voice talent, so you have to decipher what they mean.

Bill Lloyd thinks it's important to ask questions. "I'll try to sum up what I think they're trying to tell me with an adjective or two of my own and ask if that's close to what they want," he says. "If you're stuck, you can negotiate the description of your read this way."

Recently one direction I was given was, "Read it like you care, but don't care too much." The problem is, my version of caring might be different than the producer's version. It took a couple takes for me to understand what he really meant. Eventually we landed on something that worked for him, but without my ability to take his not-so-clear direction and turn it into something useful, the session would have been a lot longer and more frustrating.

While most often the director and the voice actors can understand each other, there are times when they just can't. Robyn Moler, a voice talent with a twenty-year career as the voice of some big brands, says there's a guaranteed fix for that kind of situation.

"When it's obvious I'm not giving the creatives what they want, I just ask for a line read," she says. "There's a stigma that actors don't want to be given a line reading, but I feel the opposite. I respect that the writers are hearing the line in their head a certain way, and my job is to give them what they want."

Being able to change up your reads has a lot to do with your listening skills, but it also has a lot to do with your training. And that's step number two.

STEP TWO: TRAIN

When I teach VO to beginners, on the last day of class I ask my students what they learned. The most common thing is this: they are surprised that being a voice actor involves so much more than just talking out loud.

Please don't try to get into this business until you've had some training. You will look silly. You will burn through time and money. You will fail.

Sure, record yourself imitating commercials you hear on TV and test your character voices by reading your kids to sleep at night. Go ahead and sign up to be a reader at your house of worship. But please don't try to get an agent or declare to the world that you deserve to be paid to speak without having a least a little training under your belt.

Even veteran voice actors train. Robyn Moler thinks it's important to stay fresh and diversify. "I know how to do my job, but I'm continuously trying to do it better. And honestly, I think that's a lifelong process. I also like to branch out into different genres of VO, and every work category requires a different mindset and technique. I train with professionals in that particular genre in order to practice and learn."

Bill Lloyd stays sharp by keeping in touch with other voice talent and attending "at least one weekend workshop per year." The importance of good training just can't be overstated.

This book is a guide to launching a VO career; it's not intended to teach you the skill and technique of performing as a voice talent. Those are two totally different objectives. Skills such as reading ad copy, performing promo scripts, and working in animation must be learned and developed.

Training Options

There are three options for learning how to perform in any given voice over genre, and each has pros and cons.

The main way most people pick up the skills necessary to do the job is by attending classes or working with a coach. In these settings, the tools of the trade are passed from the teacher to students through exercises, repetition, and Q&A time. Choose the right class or coach and magic can happen, with rapid progress coming from wave after wave of understanding.

If you live in a large metropolitan area, chances are there's an acting school that offers a voice over class. Here are some things to consider:

- The instructor should have lots of verifiable industry experience, either as a talent or producer.

- The instructor should be current on trends in the voice over industry. There have been huge changes in how the industry functions in the last decade, and you want to learn from someone who has witnessed them firsthand.

- The class should include an introduction to many areas of voice over: commercials, narration, corporate, promos, animation, e-learning, etc.

- Students should get a combination of lectures and on-mic practice. The more practice with feedback, the better.

- Be wary of voice over classes that funnel students into spending thousands on demos (audio résumés used by voice talent) after spending the same on multiple classes.

Unfortunately, this is also the most expensive way to train. Classes generally cost hundreds of dollars each, and coaching can cost that for a single hour. Plus, this option is dependent on where you live. If there's no reputable training near you, remote classes exist.

And that brings us to option number two.

- Many people get information on VO by looking online, and some stay there for their training. There are several providers of virtual classes and coaching, making geography irrelevant. Some offer a live group setting via video chat, others come via prerecorded courses. The cost can be the same as in-person classes, though online courses can be cheaper.

- If you're looking at purchasing a prerecorded course or live virtual class, check out the school/service provider in the same way you'd research a local class.

- Avoid coaches with results-oriented marketing. If they promise you'll have a high-paying career after you pay them thousands, run, don't walk.

- The coach should have a credible, verifiable online presence: full website with demos and work posted. Listen to everything you can find, and look them up on IMDb.com or iSpot.tv to see what they've done.

- Ask for references from their other clients, and see if they'll let you check them out. If they don't have references or won't share them with you, that's a bad sign.

- The coach should have at least five years of professional experience, be a SAG-AFTRA member (so they can have the union/nonunion conversation with you), and have their own studio setup. More on SAG-AFTRA later.

- Don't worry about geography. Just because someone is located in NYC or LA doesn't mean they're a better choice than someone who isn't. What matters most is that you click with the coach.

- Avoid coaches who tell you what you want to hear. If they overcompliment your speaking voice and paint a fabulous, rosy picture of the industry, be skeptical. My first coach didn't say a word about the quality of my voice; he was more interested in my performance.

The world of virtual voice over education is relatively new, and you should research classes carefully before investing. Understand what kind of class you're buying, and find out whether you can ask questions or get feedback. If no one's going to listen to your reads or tell you how to make them better, the class shouldn't cost anywhere near the price of a live class.

The third option is to continue doing what you're doing right now: reading the *Voice Over and Voice Acting* series of books. People thought we were crazy when we told them we were going to teach voice acting with books, but the combination of step-by-step instruction and audio files is an effective and affordable alternative to high-priced classes. No one thinks we're crazy anymore.

We have titles covering commercials, promos, and movie trailers, and we are working hard to add more genres to the series. We're also growing our library of free video tutorials.

Our authors are all accomplished full-time voice talent who audition and work every single day. Together we have over eighty years of experience in the industry. We are voices of big brands, long-running TV shows, and blockbuster video game franchises. We are all members of SAG-AFTRA, the performance union that represents the best in the business. A group like us has literally never come together to write for and educate beginning and intermediate level voice actors. The business has been very good to us, and this is our way of giving back.

When you aspire to accomplish something, it's good to hang out with people who have already done the thing you want to do. So visit Complete-Voiceover.com to see what's new.

Your Goal

However you train, beginners should have one main goal: getting the words up off the page.

When people read text from a computer screen, book, or really anything, they usually sound like they're reading. This is normal. When you were a child, if your teacher asked you to read out loud, she corrected your pronunciation. I bet she didn't correct you on your delivery.

But as a voice actor, our job is to sound not like we're reading, but like we're having thoughts coming to us at that very moment in time. It's a skill that takes time and practice to learn.

A beginner's second objective should be to work on their ability to change up their reads in response to direction. This goes back to the point I made earlier about listening. Being able to shift gears in terms of attitude, pacing, or energy is critical, since we know our first take is never going to be the one that's used.

I was once asked to add "swagger" to a read, which I thought was really strange direction because we were recording a retail read for a phone company. The script was a deal, meaning there was a product, a price, and a time limit, and not much else. It's not like there were words I could point to and say, "Okay, I'm boasting here, so I can swagger that up a bit." After asking a few questions, I figured out the director was after a kind of a frat bro attitude, so I imagined myself giving a speech after being crowned the beer pong king. She liked it. There's no way I would have deciphered a note like that unless I had training.

Lastly, training gives you the chance to learn the language of the voice over business. When a client asks you to do a set of three, or to get back on axis, or tells you they're going to grab some wild lines, they expect you to know what they're talking about. You want to show up to your jobs as prepared as possible.

STEP THREE: FIND YOUR FOCUS

The world of VO is so broad that it's pretty rare for voice talent to do it all. Sure, you can dabble in everything from e-learning to animation, but that's the shotgun method: shoot at everything and hope something falls down.

There's an old proverb that goes like this: "The man who chases two rabbits catches none."

This is good to keep in mind, especially when you're just beginning your training. Voice actors work in over a dozen distinct categories of the industry, each with its own set of rules and techniques. It's overwhelming to think you'll have to train for all of them if you want a career.

Don't worry about that right now. Find the rabbit you want to catch, learn the best way to catch it, and go hunting. When you nab it, find another rabbit.

Most voice talent first learn on commercial scripts. The traditional thirty-second TV spot isn't the king of advertising like it once was, but it's still a huge revenue generator for many voice talent. You definitely want to know how to read commercials.

But reads that are appropriate for commercials will be wildly off base for long-form narration. Likewise, if you deliver promo copy like you would a script for a phone system, you're going to sound completely bananas. So at some point, you'll need to familiarize yourself with other areas of the business.

The More You Learn, The More You Earn

Here's a list of the most active corners of the VO world along with a sample script for each one. You can hear them by downloading the free audio files at Complete-Voiceover.com. All of these scripts are based on actual projects. I tweaked the language and used our fictional client, "Harry's," which you'll see throughout. The result will give you an idea of what each kind of script looks like.

TV/Radio Commercials

This category needs no introduction. They're the 30-, 60-, or 120-second spots we see on TV, online, and hear on radio/streaming every day. Despite all you may have heard about the decline in TV advertising, commercials aren't going anywhere. They still represent most of the big money jobs in VO. Talent can earn six figures from one good commercial client, though those jobs are tough to land. Difficult or not, any voice talent hoping to earn money has to be good at interpreting ad copy.

TV script:
Example 3a

Can inspiration make your heart stop, and your pulse race at the same time?

Yes.

Can a 340 Horsepower V8 provide both raw acceleration and intelligent fuel economy?

Yes.

And can all this style and engineering be yours for under 35 thousand?

Absolutely.

The all new Blizzard, from Harry's. We engineer better rides.

Radio script:
Example 3b

There you are.

Sitting in the box seats of a home game.

You have an ice cold soda in one hand and a big hot pretzel in the other,

and you think to yourself, "This is the way it should be."

But this perfect little slice of life can cost a small fortune.

That soda? Nine fifty. The pretzel? More than any pretzel has a right to cost.

Those tickets? Don't even ask.

Luckily, there's a place you can get a big league experience without the big league price tag.

This spring, baseball is coming to town in a big way.

Join Shriner County's newest residents, The Cougars at Shriner Park, beginning in March.

Home stands, home runs, and hassle-free family fun.

Opening day is April 3rd. Ticket packages available online at ShrinerCougars.com.

Or call 877-Cougars.

Baseball the way it was meant to be.

Corporate Narration

Production companies of all sizes are hired by corporations to produce content. Videos are made for training, marketing, informing, and for social media. Many of them have voices. One day you might narrate a video training retail employees on customer service, and the next you'll work on one showing pharmaceutical reps how to convince doctors to prescribe a new drug.

Corporate narration is sometimes tricky because often you're talking about subjects you don't know anything about. There can be lots of acronyms, odd turns of phrase, and corporate-speak. Many scripts are not written to be spoken but lifted from a printed manual or web copy. Being able to see through all of it and clearly deliver the message is definitely a skill that'll help you get hired again and again.

Example 3c

Now that you know what to look for in a potential case of hydrocarbon poisoning and how to treat it with HCP-Kit, here are a few more things to keep in mind. Caution should be exercised in administering other antidotes with HCP-Kit, as safety has not been established. If the decision is made to administer another antidote with HCP-Kit, the drug should not be introduced concurrently in the same IV line. HCP-Kit is incompatible with thiosulfate, sodium nitrate, and certain acids.

Promos

TV networks and affiliates run promos advertising their programming. Typically, promos air for a short time, however, there are exceptions. Some networks have one voice that does pretty much every promo. Others hire talent just for certain uses, like one for their sports division and another for just their drama lineup. Sometimes individual shows have their own promo voices. Also, shows that go into syndication will be sold with the promos already written and recorded. So a talent can book an entire package and voice multiple promos for every episode of a show.

Example 3d

Tonight we're bringing you the best comedies on television.

With the all-time best episodes of Harry's Place.

Then on That Other Show

Lucy enters the invention convention

But things don't go according to plan.

Tonight starting at 7.

Radio ID/Imaging

This is the work that identifies local radio stations. Fun fact: in the United States, by law the FCC requires radio stations to identify themselves at the top of every hour. Often stations will have their on-air talent record these, but there are fewer and fewer local talent these days, so this work is hired out to voice talent. Typically, you'll record a package of several IDs at one time.

Example 3e

Commercials off. Music on. Now 10 at the top of the hour. On the all new 104.9 Blink FM.

Animation/Video Games

Pretty self-explanatory. The more character voices you can do, the better. Producers like to hire as few talent as possible, so the more characters they can get out of you, the more likely you are to be hired.

Video Game Script:
Example 3f

Phrases:

Fame AND fortune. I want it all!

You just don't know what's good for you!

Prepare to be plundered!

I've waited for this for a looooooong tiiiime!

Efforts:

Punching another human.

Taking a punch from another human.

Short panic reaction from being shot at.

Animation Script:
Example 3g

Son: I'm sad because I can't go to my sleepover!

Dad: Well, you don't want to get typhus, do you?

Son: What's typhus?

Dad: I don't know, but I think it makes you go blind.

Son: Ya think?

Dad: I don't know, I just know Mom wouldn't want you to go to that house.

Son: I miss Mom.

Dad: Yeah. Me too.

Son: Aw nuts. Just got coffee on my new shirt.

Long-Form/Series Narration

Documentary and series narration is a special art that is mostly cast by producers in Los Angeles or New York, but not always. The subject matter will always influence the choice of talent. If you sound like a rough and tough Southern good ol' boy, you'll be great for shows like *River Monsters*, but you're not likely to narrate that documentary on the Great Recession. This kind of narration is storytelling at its most obvious. There are usually three acts to the show, each with its own goals and tone, and the talent has to recognize them and treat them accordingly.

Example 3h

By all accounts, the Millers are an average suburban family. Two kids. Two cars. A new home in a quiet suburban neighborhood. They've just bought a slice of the American dream.

But it doesn't take long for the dream to turn into a nightmare.

Not long after moving in, the Millers begin to notice things. Books rearranged on shelves. Fresh cut flowers die overnight.

And perhaps most unnerving, they hear what sounds like a quiet vibration that doesn't seem to have a source.

With no apparent explanation for these happenings, the Millers contact ghost hunter Rob Lewis, locally famous for his claims that emerging technology developed by his company entice paranormal entities into communicating with the living.

This is the story of what happens next.

Education/E-learning

A lot of learning has moved online, for better or worse, and most of it needs voice talent. Typically, students are propped in front of their screens, clicking through a course. They could be patients learning what to expect from a medical procedure or mechanics learning about various systems in new cars. It's tempting for talent to take an academic approach to these reads because the scripts are usually pretty dry. But that's a trap that will bore your audience and not earn you any repeat business. The trick with this kind of work is to make it as interesting as possible, so you can keep your audience engaged.

Example 3i

Welcome to Learning Link, a continuing education resource for HR professionals worldwide.

In this training, we're going back to basics on a difficult subject: harassment and

nondiscrimination.

Every organization has their own antiharassment and antidiscrimination policies, yet it's worth revisiting them on a regular basis. Various policies may use different language, but the goal is always the same: to ensure a safe, respectful, and welcoming workplace.

Let's begin with a brief review of the law. We'll start with the term "harassment."

Audiobooks

The market for audiobooks has exploded in the last few years with double-digit annual growth. For beginners, ACX.com is the best way to get started as a narrator. Owned by Amazon, it's a marketplace that pairs narrators with independent authors who need someone to record their books.

This work takes a tremendous amount of time and storytelling chops. One hour of finished audio could take five to ten hours of work to produce, so a novel that's ten hours long could mean recording for fifty hours or more.

Example 3j

I first met Tommy Watson in the musty basement of St. Mark's Medical Center among the rows of tall steel shelving piled high with dusty file boxes. He was in a section marked "1972."

Looking back on it now, he was way too easy to find. But that didn't matter at the time because I let my anticipation get away from me.

When I saw him, I got really excited. I approached him quietly, breath quickening, nervous tension seizing my hands so much that I dropped my flashlight. I wanted to know everything about him, but it was critical that I wasn't obvious about it.

That wasn't going to be a problem because I was pretty good at this. Discoveries like these were what I lived for. That point in the hunt where, after all the searching, you've found that which you think you've been looking for. The possibilities began bouncing through my mind even before I knew anything about my new friend. A new life. A renewed sense of privacy. Another challenge ahead, one I was definitely up to. This was a rush.

One of the overhead lights flickered and went out with a sharp click as soon as I hunkered down next to him. The already dim basement now a little more so, which was just fine by me. Somewhere down a hall, a pipe clanked.

IVR Systems/Phonecasting/Storecasting

Interactive voice response systems (those voice recognition systems you hear when you call banks, utility companies, and such) are an interesting challenge to voice talent because they require very technical reads.

Phrases are broken up and reordered by a computer depending on statements made by the caller, so voice talent have to record phrases multiple times with different inflections. Phonecasting is basically advertising on hold, and storecasting is mostly used by grocery stores with prerecorded minicommercials about sales and promotions being played over the store's speakers.

Example 3k

Project: IVR System

Sorry, I didn't understand. You want to make a payment, is that right? If yes, press one. If no, press two. If you need to return to the main menu, press pound.

Voice Matching

Sometimes a toy, book, or video game is made with a licensed character from a movie or TV show, and instead of having the original talent record the audio, the producer will hire a replacement who sounds just like the character. Often this is an economic decision, but sometimes it's because of availability of the original voice actor. For example, Tom Hanks voiced Woody in the *Toy Story* movies, but many toys and other products with Woody's voice are done by Hanks's younger brother, Jim. A friend of mine is the voice of "Older Han Solo" in the Star Wars universe because Harrison Ford doesn't have time to do VO.

Example 3l
Reference: Ryan Seacrest

Phrases:

Coming up!

And next!

You're a winner!

Looping/ADR/Dubbing

Looping, ADR (Automated Dialogue Replacement), and dubbing are ways voice talent can support the creation of TV shows and movies. If a shot has a crowd, usually that crowd would make noise. But when the scene was shot, chances are the background actors were told to be silent, so the sound department could pick up the main actors' dialogue. The crowd's audio needs to be re-created by a loop group, which is a bunch of actors brought into the studio to record the crowd scene. ADR usually refers to the replacement of dialogue by the actor who said it on set, but in animation, voice actors are sometimes hired to add additional vocal elements to a dialogue track. Dubbing involves replacing a project's language with another. All this kind of work only happens in places with a huge postproduction industry, like Los Angeles.

Example 3m
The scene: a park.
The activity: parents playing with kids.

Here are some possible phrases:

There you go, you're getting it.

Try throwing underhand this time.

Who else wants to play catch?

Come on kids, time to go.

Gadget/Product VO

No joke, I'm the voice of a treadmill. There's a company that makes a line of fitness equipment with the option of having a personal trainer guide you through your workout. You can pick the gender of your trainer, and if you pick the guy, you get me barking at you. Digital assistants are getting more popular, and they all have voices, as does infotainment systems in cars. We'll see a lot more of this stuff in the future.

Example 3n
Product: A treadmill.

When you're ready, press the red start button to begin.

We're going to start out slow with a gentle warm up, then increase our speed and intensity.

Warming up signals your body to get ready for a higher level of activity, protecting it from injury.

Wouldn't want to pull a hammy.

Movie Trailers

If you picture the voice over business as a pyramid with the most common types of work at the bottom and the least common at the top, movie trailers would be the tiniest bit at the peak. Trailer voices are mostly male, always well paid, and very small in number. There just aren't that many because trailer pros are regarded as the industry's elite performers. As such, it takes a lot of time to work in this genre.

Landing a trailer or movie campaign means the voice actor has spent years trying to reach the top of their game. VO artists sometimes do a lot of promo work on their way to the very exclusive world of trailers.

Example 30

Critics are raving

The Red Desk

Is hilarious and heartfelt

The best movie I've seen this year

The Red Desk

Rated R

STEP FOUR: INVEST IN GEAR

When I started my career, I'd get an audition from my agent, drive to an office belonging to the agent, the advertising agency, or a casting director, and be handed a piece of paper containing the audition copy.

After having a minute to look it over, I'd go into a recording booth where someone else would sit behind a glass wall in a control room filled with equipment that cost more than our family's cars, and that person would press buttons and slide faders as I read the copy, recording it onto physical tape, which would be spinning on a separate machine. I'd have one take to get it right, maybe two if they heard something they wanted to tweak. Then I'd leave, never hearing the recording, and I'd wait to see if I was booked. The only gear that belonged to me was the water bottle I brought in, except I usually forgot it in the car.

Today, that kind of scenario almost never happens. The task of auditioning for work has shifted to the voice talent, who are all expected to have recording setups at home. That means we all have to invest in equipment.

The good news is that you don't need much, and it's a lot more affordable than it used to be. But there are a few basics you just can't live without: a computer with recording software, a microphone, and a quiet place to record.

Your Computer

I'm certainly no tech wizard, so I'm going to keep this simple. You can record audio using just about any computer made in the last five years. As long as it has a USB port, you can get live sound into that machine. Once it's there, you can use a number of audio editors to perfect your auditions.

At first, just use what you have, but avoid the temptation to rely on your smartphone or tablet for your primary recording setup. A lot of talent do this when they're first getting started because everyone has a phone. That's fine while you're learning but when you start auditioning for actual work, audio quality matters even when you're new.

Not long ago it was common for people to use phones to record auditions. But expectations have gone up, and now we often see "No iPhone auditions" written on audition copy. Talent buyers gave us some time to figure out this new world of recording ourselves, but now that we have, they're picky. They want clean audio at an even level, not just because it sounds good but because sometimes they can use the audition in the final job. More than once my audition has been lifted into a project, which is great because I didn't have to actually do the job, and I still got paid.

Listen to Example 4a to hear the difference in sound quality between a phone and a computer.

Recording on a mobile device can be your backup, though their internal microphones aren't high quality. You can find external mics and various adaptors to connect them, and these can greatly increase the quality of the file. But currently, even a high-end microphone connected to a phone is a victim of the processing in that recording device. Things just tend to sound better when they're recorded using a computer.

There's an abundance of recording software out there, some of it easier to learn than others. If you have a Mac, try out Garage Band, which comes free with your OS. Windows users can try Sound Editor. I'm going to recommend two other options: one free and one paid.

My favorite free audio editor is Audacity, which can be downloaded for either Mac or Windows at www.audacityteam.org. This is a solid bit of software accompanied by a wealth of online training and tutorials making it easy to set up and learn. It won't be long before you realize it does way more than what you need it to do.

Pro tip: the current version of Audacity doesn't automatically allow you to save your auditions as mp3 files, the format the industry wants when you submit an audition. You need to take the extra step of configuring it to do so. The website has clear instructions for this, and it only takes a minute. Pro tip number two: always record voice over auditions in mono, not stereo.

A great paid audio editor is Twisted Wave, at www.twistedwave. com. It makes recording and editing super easy. If you're on a Mac, you can download the software if you want, but you can also run it in a browser window without downloading anything at all, a good choice for Windows users.

Robyn Moler uses Twisted Wave. "I had the app on my iPad and iPhone for recording when I was away from home, and I liked that it's an easy program to use, so I got it for my desktop. I pair it with software called Izotope RX, which cleans up audio by removing any clicks or anomalies."

There's one other editor I want to mention because if you're doing any research about home recording, you're going to hear the name. The industry standard for recording nearly anything, from music to VO to cinematic scores, is Pro Tools.

Made by my friends at Avid (full disclosure - I've worked for them in the past), it's the gold standard built for professionals. Some voice talent use it to record at home, but as capable as it is, I think it's overkill for the needs of beginning voice talent. It's pretty slick though, and if you'd like to try it out, they make a free version called ProTools|First. Find it at Avid.com.

Your Microphone

I'm going to assume that the sky is not the limit when it comes to how much money you want to invest in this new career. If you're tempted to throw a lot of money at a microphone thinking the more you spend, the better you'll sound, I'd hold off on that.

The quality of your recordings will depend on a lot of things, and your choice of mic is just one of them. Your whole system will act as one, and if you've got one bit of gear that's vastly better than the rest, its quality will be dragged down by the other components in your setup. So avoid the temptation to spend all you've got on a microphone.

There are lots of resources to help you choose a mic. YouTube has some fantastic VO channels. Check out VOBuzz Weekly, Booth Junkie, and Edge Studio. They cover all kinds of gear, mics included. The reviews on Amazon.com, BHPhotovideo.com, and MusiciansFriend.com are also good places to research mics.

I'm going to recommend three options: one each for small, medium, and large budgets.

USB mics are the least expensive way to start. There is a wide variety to choose from, and they get their name from their ability to connect to your computer's USB port. All should be plug-and-play, so you can get up and running in no time.

A USB mic requires no other equipment for basic recording needs other than maybe a pop filter (which helps reduce popping and breath noises) and a mic stand to hold it in place. They provide decent sound for about $100, yet you will find plenty of people who will disagree with that.

Personally, I think they're perfect for talent who are just starting to learn. When I used a USB mic, my choice was one made by AudioTechnica, an older version of a mic that's known today as the AT2020. It's a great starter mic used by a lot of newer voice talent.

When you're ready for something more professional, you'll step up to microphones that connect to your computer using an XLR cable. The three-pinned XLR connector is not something you've likely seen before, unless you happen to work with high-end audio or video. Don't go looking for a place to plug it into your computer; you won't find one. It connects through another bit of gear called an audio interface that sits in between the mic and your computer.

An interface converts the live audio signal coming into the microphone (your voice) to a digital signal your computer can recognize. Most interfaces also provide power to XLR mics because most microphones in this category don't have a power source of their own.

Your choice of interface can be limited by your recording software. Some interfaces play nice with certain audio editors but not with others. Some also come with their own software, though many of these editors lack features, usability, stability, or all three. So if you've decided on editing software, check the developer's website to see which interfaces they recommend.

I use a Focusrite Scarlett 2i2, a little red box with two mic inputs, 48-volt phantom power, nice-sounding internal preamps (software that treats the audio signal before it goes to the computer), and it's compatible with Audacity. Setup was easy, and it's more than enough for my needs, and I suspect for yours too.

The mic choice of many established voice talent is the Sennheiser MKH-416 shotgun microphone. At around $1,000, this mic isn't cheap, but it offers a lot of benefits. First, it has a bright sound that works well for commercials and promos because it allows the voice to cut through music and sound design. I think it just sounds great. You can always find people who disagree, but its superior sound is just one reason why the VO community has relied on it for decades.

The 416 makes no noise of its own, unlike some cheaper mics, which can ruin recordings with low-level hisses or hums. It's also super rugged because it was originally designed to record location sound on film and TV sets. The thing I like about it is that it's a directional mic. It records sound coming from just one place, the direction in which you point it.

We'll talk about your recording space in a minute, but a lot of home studios aren't exactly acoustically perfect. They can be noisy and filled with echoes or other acoustic anomalies that drag down the quality of the final product. A directional mic helps to lessen the impact of this kind of thing and automatically cleans up the audio before it reaches your computer, within reason. It's not going to help if you're recording in your tiled bathroom. But it can smooth out audio bumps if you take the time to make your recording space ready to record sound.

This directionality also allows you to play around with your reads. Speaking directly into the mic, also known as working "on axis," produces a different effect than speaking off to the side, or "off axis." You can also adjust the volume of the signal going into the mic by simply moving closer or farther away from it. Want an intimate read?

Get right up close so that your lips are nearly touching the windscreen. Need to do some shouting? Back way off from the mic.

Another great thing about the 416 is that it holds its value. There's a robust secondary market for them because they will always be in demand, and they don't really change over time. If you need to sell in the future, you'll be able to get back most of your investment.

There are certainly plenty of other XLR mics at or below this price point to consider, including the Neumann TLM-102 and -103, the AKG C-214 and -414 (which have directional settings), and the Rode NTG-2. Do your research and know that there probably isn't a bad choice, but there are mics that are more suited to certain kinds of VO than to other recording tasks. Read some reviews and go from there.

If money is no object, you won't find a voice talent that wouldn't take a Neumann U-87 if you gave them one. It's the granddaddy of all studio mics and the gold standard in most professional recording studios. It's also overkill for VO, but if you simply must have the best, the U-87 is probably the one to get.

A U-87 will run you $4,000 new, but you might be able to pick up a used one for maybe half that. I would strongly suggest you don't choose this mic unless you have very high quality components in the rest of your setup. Having this kind of mic patched through with cheap cables to an inferior preamp is like putting $10,000 worth of rims and tires on a car that's worth $5,000 on a good day.

Which mic is best for you? The one you have. This is especially true at the beginning of your career. More than almost any other piece of gear, it's possible to get overly technical and geek out over each microphone's specs and attributes, and there are plenty of voice talent who like to argue for one mic over another. In the end, they all get the job done.

Your Recording Space

Having a dedicated recording space is pretty critical to a VO career. You'll need to carve out a spot in your house that's free from noise coming from inside and outside. Bathrooms and laundry areas are usually bad; walk-in closets are ideal. If you have an extra bedroom, that'll work for your home studio as long as you're able to make it a dead space.

Audio engineers talk about rooms as being dead, which are free from echoes and other audio anomalies, and live, which are rooms that allow sound to bounce around, producing noise in addition to the source (your voice). You need a dead space because otherwise your auditions will have unclear audio, and your chances of booking anything will be next to zero. Dirty, echo-filled auditions get deleted.

I was curious about the percentage of talent submitting auditions that are flawed by echoes, or low levels, or otherwise not up to industry standards. To find out, I called a friend of mine, a senior copywriter at a big advertising agency. He had just wrapped a large project that required a female VO, and out of the eighty auditions he heard, a solid dozen of them were technically bad enough that he didn't even bother listening. He doesn't want to be identified, but his message to talent was pretty brutal.

"Bad recordings just make me think it's going to take hours of working with you in the session to get the read right," he says. "Your audition might be magical, but if I can't hear it well, it tells me you submitted without listening to it first. If I can hear some good bits I'll sometimes request another file, but usually I just move on. It's cold but it's true."

Remember, even if you're not yet a seasoned pro, it's still important to sound like one. You're trying to establish credibility with decision makers, and submitting auditions with bad audio isn't the way to do it.

Luckily, your recording space doesn't have to be a completely enclosed room. I've seen people get creative and build convertible recording areas where the space around the mic is isolated with sound-absorbing material like moving blankets. As long as you have power, light, and it's quiet, you can make it work this way.

Turning a live room into a dead space requires some thinking. For one thing, some computers can be quite noisy. Desktops are usually worse than laptops, but some portable machines are pretty loud. The way around this is to get the offending box out of the booth, or at least far enough away that it won't be picked up by the mic. Desktop boxes can be moved outside of a walk-in closet, and long cables can be used to connect a monitor in the booth so you can operate it from afar. Bluetooth mice and keyboards are great replacements for their wired counterparts.

The other thing to look at is the sound quality of your space itself. You will likely need some kind of sound absorption material, like Auralux, or panels and bass traps sold by GIK Acoustics. When you record anything, be it an audition or a job, you don't want any sound in the background at all if you can help it. No whir of air conditioning, no clank of radiators in the winter, no leaf blowers or traffic noise from outside, nothing. I know a VO guy who didn't buy a house he loved because it backed up to a Whole Foods, and he knew the rumbling delivery trucks would screw up his takes. While there's software available to help mitigate background noise, too much ambient sound can be an home-recording killer.

Our first home studio was a walk-in closet, and if we had a closet large enough in our current house, we'd probably be using it. Instead, we built a booth. You can have a look at it on my YouTube channel.

Speaking of YouTube, plenty of people have posted videos on how to build booths on the cheap using moving blankets, foam mattress toppers, PVC pipe, and all kinds of other creative solutions. Check them out if you're on a microbudget.

Our booth is a custom solution, but if you don't have someone local who can build you one, there are lots of companies selling isolation booths online. Like ordering anything else, you place the order and they ship it to your home. They come with pros and cons.

You can't beat the convenience of buying a ready-made booth. When you place your order, just choose the booth size and features you want. Need a hardwood floor and a door with a window? No problem. Pretty much anything can be done, for a price. When the booth arrives you can assemble it yourself. The manufacturers provide detailed instructions so you can be up and running as soon as you install your gear.

When you buy a booth, that's exactly what you get. You don't get any other gear. You pay for four walls, a door, a floor, and a ceiling, and unless you upgrade your order, that's what arrives. Preinstalled audio treatment on the interior, windows, and lighting kits are just a few possible add-ons.

As you can imagine, the big drawback to these booths is their price. They're not cheap, even at the low end. You're looking at a minimum of $1,500 for a bare-bones unit with no way to get fresh air inside. And the sky's the limit, though $5,000 will buy you a very nice booth with a lot of bells and whistles.

Most booths, regardless of price, generally sound pretty rough on their own. You literally sound like you're talking inside a box, which you are. No one hires talent who sound like that, so you should plan on treating the interior with acoustic panels and bass traps. This additional equipment will make the booth sound great but will add to the overall cost of the project. It's something most people forget to work into the budget.

The other thing about booths: they're difficult to move. Once they're up and running, they're a pain to break down. If you plan on moving frequently, I'd skip the booth and figure out another place to record.

Three established names in isolation booths are WhisperRoom.com, StudioBricks.com, and VocalBooth.com. You can also check Craigslist or NextDoor.com for used booths. They come up pretty frequently, especially in big cities.

If buying a booth sounds too expensive, there are lots of creative DIY booth solutions out there. Honestly, when you're just beginning to learn the craft, don't worry about the quality of your recordings; worry more about the quality of your reads.

At this point, investing in learning materials like books and courses is far more important than your gear. If no one but your teachers are going to hear your recordings, then it really doesn't matter where you record them.

All the fancy gear in the world will not save you from doing a bad audition if you don't know how to read the script and tell a story while doing it. Think of it like this: Do expensive running shoes make you faster? If you're an elite athlete, maybe. But for the rest of us, no, they do not.

So train and learn, and *then* think about gear that'll help your auditions stand up to industry standards.

STEP FIVE: BUILD DEMOS

All voice talent, whether you're still waiting for your first booking or you've been in business for decades, must have voice demos available online. Sure, you can join a VO membership site (more on that in Step 6) and begin auditioning without a demo, but to earn any meaningful amount of credibility in this business, a demo is a must.

A demo is about a minute's worth of audio that showcases what you can do with a certain type of work. Virtually all talent have a commercial demo. Many also have others for work like promos, animation, narration, and so on. It's not a good idea to blend demos. The audience for a commercial demo is much different than animation, so to have both styles of work in one demo just makes everyone hit the stop button.

Who listens to demos? Agents. Potential clients. Anyone who is considering working with you will want to hear what they're getting before they make a decision. So the most important thing about a demo is that it's an honest representation of where your skills are right now. Want to kill your chances of working? Show a producer one thing in your demo and then be totally incapable of doing it in the session. No one likes the bait and switch.

A lot of things can be faked with demos, which is why decision makers don't completely trust them, especially with talent they haven't heard before. Hence, most agents and producers will ask for an audition instead of hiring you off your demo.

Still, without a demo, your career will be dead before it begins.

So what does a good demo sound like? It depends on the work category. As an example, you can listen to mine at ChrisAgos.com. You can also google "voice talent" and find dozens of voice actors' sites to browse. Or, visit the site of a talent agency that represents voice over talent. Many post demos, and it's likely that when you get representation, your agent will post yours.

Just about everyone has a commercial demo, and I think it should be the first you tackle, so let's start there. Think of your demo as a collection of your greatest hits. Demos should contain four to six short clips of different scripts totaling about a minute in length when edited all together.

You want to find copy that sits well with your age, voice type, and overall ability level. Then put your best reads together, leading with your very best, and by best I mean the one that best represents what you bring to the table as a voice talent. You also want to make sure the products and subject matter are timely. It's not a good idea to include copy written for a product or company that no longer exists.

There are two competing philosophies about how to build a good commercial demo. Some people think variety is best. That is, you should include a bunch of reads you can reliably pull off: confident and reassuring, intelligent yet whimsical, ironic yet knowledgeable, smart but relatable, and so on. In the old days, when there were only a handful of working VO talent, those who could bounce from one read style to another were in high demand.

The other school of thought centers on sticking with a signature sound, one style that is quintessentially you. The idea is when producers want that sound, they'll think of you instead of trying to get someone else to sound just like you. Proponents of this line of thinking argue there are so many people in the business now that talent are no longer expected to be vocal chameleons.

I'm not entirely sure I agree with that, but I can see the point: be you and the work will come. Try to be too many things, and producers won't know what to do with you. I'll leave it up to you and whomever trains you to decide which philosophy to stick with.

The Rules

I have a couple rules for demos in all categories. Here they are:

Rule 1: Do not produce your own demo.
Rule 2: See rule number one.

It's very tempting to think that you not only could, but actually should, produce your own demo, particularly if you're hoping to spend as little as possible on start-up costs. You've got a mic and a computer, your own labor is free, and you might even have some training. Why not do you own demo?

Because generally, humans aren't good at evaluating their own work, especially if they're new to a skill. I can almost guarantee that tackling the organization and production of your own demos will make you sound more like a beginner than if you had some help.

For example, a lot of self-produced demos open with the talent introducing themselves, something done only by people who don't know that you should never do this. A proper professional demo only contains audio samples of your work. Including anything else marks you as inexperienced. Remember, you want to give the impression that you're a knowledgeable professional, even if you're not quite there yet. Working with a pro will help avoid these kinds of mistakes.

I've listened to hundreds of demos over the years, and I'm convinced that having a second, knowledgeable set of ears makes a huge difference in the sound and feel of a demo.

To create a good demo:

- Find and choose appropriate, well-written pieces of copy
- Analyze and develop reads for each
- Record the full spots
- Produce the full spots, which involves picking music (watch out for copyright violations) and developing sound design
- Choose which chunks of each spot to use for the demo
- Choose a running order
- Edit the chunks down to about a minute in length
- Listen critically to make sure the order makes sense
- Make corrections if something seems off
- Master the final demo to even out volume peaks and valleys

If you're new to this business, you're not going to get a better result doing all this on your own. I know a guy who's an audio engineer by trade, and even he had help putting his first demo together.

So plan on finding someone to help you. It doesn't have to be a demo production service, though if you come across one you like and the price doesn't seem outrageous, that's an option. If you have a teacher or coach you like, they're likely to be willing. Other voice talent are possibly good candidates, but only if they're very experienced.

As you start thinking about your own demo, listen to as many as you can, but focus on ones that are in your gender and age range. This will give you an idea of which read styles are in fashion at the moment. Finally, listening to other talents' demos helps you find people in the business you can look up to. You want to have something to aim for.

Every part of demo production is important, but probably the most important aspect is the running order. Most people aren't going to listen to the whole thing, so it's important to put your best stuff first. When you're new to the business, this means choosing the read that best represents you, the one that's really in your sweet spot. Whomever you're training with can help you define what that is.

If you're looking to produce multiple demos, do your homework and listen to those of established talent in whatever category you'd like to work in. Video game demos sound much different than radio imaging demos.

The last thing I'll say about demos is that timing is everything. It's tempting to take a class, put together a demo, and send it out there. However, I'd say the biggest mistake new talent make is putting together their demo too soon.

I know you're interested in this, and you want to get it up and running ASAP. You want a return on your investment, and quick. But jumping into a demo before you're ready could hinder your chances of making this work.

I did my first demo too early. I took ten private lessons, then recorded a demo that I hope never, ever sees the light of day again. I really didn't know what I was doing, and you can hear it through the entire two minutes and thirty seconds. Yes. It was two-and-a-half times longer than today's demos.

I sent that demo to every talent buyer I could imagine, and wouldn't you know it? I didn't get much of a response. My first paid VO job came through my teacher, who referred me to a producer friend of his. I had one line in a radio commercial. I was elated, but I didn't really earn it. I got it through a relationship.

A year later, I recorded a far better demo. Because I spent a ton of time listening to what was being broadcast, I was much stronger. I leaned into my strengths and tried to stay away from my weak points.

Eventually, I got an agent and started booking a few things. But I can't help but wonder how many people passed on me because of that first demo. It's cliché, but it's true: you never have a second chance to make a good first impression.

I'll never know if I missed out on work because of the inferior quality of my first demo. But I do know that it took me a year of listening and practice to really learn how to deliver copy.

If you simply must make your own demo, I want you to at least know how the pros do them. So I'm writing a separate book about how to build amazing demos in any VO genre, and it might be available by the time you read this. Check complete-voiceover.com for updates.

Once you have a fully produced demo, or even a couple of them, you'll need to make it available. The best way to do this is to post it online. But how and where can you get the word out?

STEP SIX: MARKET

Historically, voice talent have marketed themselves to a very small group: ad agency copywriters and producers. Old timers tell stories of hanging out in the lobbies of advertising agency office buildings. Writers would come down, see someone they knew and say, "Hey, let's do a couple radio spots."

If only it was that easy today. The list of potential employers is much longer, and voiceover marketing has broadened along with it.

I like to think of marketing as a three-pronged effort: things you can do, things an agent can do, and things a membership to a VO site can do.

Things You Can Do

Having a website devoted exclusively to your VO work is an important start. If you have another job and a site to showcase that work, don't be tempted to post your demos alongside your other career. You want your voice acting material to stand alone under a different URL.

Here's why: whenever a voice talent is hired by anyone—an ad agency, a video game producer, a TV network or production company— it's expensive. They're not only paying the talent but the director/

producer, writers, audio engineers, and a host of other people. There's also the cost of developing the project up to that point.

It's not cheap. Because of this, there's a high degree of trust that has to come with booking any voice actor, known or unknown. Trust comes from credibility, and credibility starts with a good demo and solid audition, but another big part of the equation is perception. That's where your website comes in.

Imagine you're looking for a new dentist. You go online, check out some reviews, and click on a couple links. You see a bunch of sites filled with smiling people and glowing testimonials. But on one dentist's site, you find information on tennis coaching along side the toothy grins of his patients. Turns out this dentist is also very good at teaching high school kids how to play well enough to get college scholarships.

Huh. Do you want this guy working on your smile? I don't. I want my dentist to be interested in nothing other than making sure my teeth don't fall out of my head.

That's what talent buyers want from their voice actors. They want to know your only goal is to do their job the right way. If you're also a graphic designer, quilter, or nutritionist, those things aren't important to them. One exception is if you also have an active on-camera acting career. Feel free to include VO on that website because everyone assumes voice talent are really just actors anyway.

I can hear some of you saying, "I don't need a whole site, I can just send some mp3s or Soundcloud links." Well, yeah, but don't you think some clients are going to look you up? You might have an easier time getting them to trust you if you have a solid VO-based web presence.

While we're on the subject of trust, that copywriter I mentioned earlier? During our conversation, he said something really interesting. He thinks of the whole casting process as one giant audition. Talent are auditioning for the job, but the writer wants to do a good job for the other creatives, and the whole team wants to do well for the client.

Changes happen pretty fast in any industry, but advertising can be brutal. One decision can cause entire teams to be cut as clients shift work to other agencies. Voice over is a team sport, and everyone has to trust everyone else to do their best work at all times.

Once you have a couple bookings under your belt, following up with clients is a great way to build repeat business. If you're easy to work with and do a good job, they'll hire you again, especially if you're keeping your name front and center on a regular basis.

One way I used to do this was through a monthly newsletter, which makes me sound like I'm a million years old. But yeah, I got started when I was really young and not everyone had email. So once a month I'd sit down at my computer and use some awful desktop publishing software to churn out a two-page document filled with "articles" on what I was working on. I'd write about anything I booked and profiled production companies who hired me. I'd mention where to see or hear those jobs, and if I didn't have enough material to fill two pages, I'd write jokes or do silly top ten lists.

This might sound cringe-inducing, but it worked really well. I sent newsletters to every agent in my market, even the ones that didn't represent me. I wanted them to know that I was booking jobs their talent were missing out on. Anyone who ever auditioned or hired me got a newsletter. Whether they read every word or pitched it sight unseen, they saw my name. Repetition breeds familiarity.

I did this for five years, and by the time I stopped, I was with the talent agents I wanted to be with and had a nice roster of repeat business. I also had people asking where the newsletters went. They kind of missed getting them every month.

Be strategic about how you keep in touch with people. Obviously, in today's world we keep in touch via social media, blogs, and email blasts. Keep posts brief; give shout-outs to and/or tag the recording studios and production companies you worked with on a job. And if a big brand hires you, don't place a ton of emphasis on them. You don't want to allow huge national names to upstage your personal brand.

Besides, having those brands in your marketing tends to alienate potential employers who work with competing brands. Coke won't be eager to hire you if they know you've worked for Pepsi.

Robyn Moler took her marketing to a fun level. "I used to buy boxes of fortune cookies from a promotional company and have the fortune say something like, 'For some good ad fortune, hire Robyn Moler as your VO.' I packed them in these cute Chinese carryout boxes and handed them out at sessions. People seemed to like them."

But as the business changed, her marketing had to change with it. "I started to get fewer and fewer sessions where the agency folks were in the same city as I was. And then the cookies got stale and gross until I just threw them away."

"Today," she says, "I send holiday cards to producers I've worked for, and if I get a big win, I'll send a gift of some kind to the creative team. For example, when I was the voice of Aldi, I shipped a big box of Aldi snacks to the agency. The producers were bummed there wasn't an Aldi close to the agency, so I wanted to share some of the client's treats with them."

However you reach out, have a reason to do so, especially if you're doing it via email. Don't just ask people to hire you again. Inform them of something, offer to help, or connect with them on LinkedIn. Stay in touch by giving them something of value.

Things a Voiceover Agent Can Do

The question of whether or not you need, or should try to get, an agent is one you'll have to consider at some point.

You can think of talent agents as the gatekeepers of a lot of the world's high-paying voice over work. An agent sits between the client and the actors and tries to match the client's needs with talent who fit. The agent also represents the talent's interests when they book that job.

Your agent will get the job details and make sure you have everything you need to do the job: location, time, rate, etc. In exchange for the introduction to that client, the job coordination, and possibly negotiation of the rate, the agent gets a commission. Usually it's 10–15 percent of your fee. Sometimes that's paid by the client, and other times it's paid by you.

Do you need an agent? Probably, though there's no easy answer for everyone. There are voice talent who work without agents and take pride in being able to have a career without paying commissions. But the majority of talent find having an agent is hugely beneficial to their career progress and earning potential.

When you sign with an agent, they'll begin to include you on the auditions that come through their agency. Most agents rep voice actors for everything under the sun, so you'll be able to audition for all kinds of work from commercials to animation to narration. Some agencies are stronger in certain areas than others, though. If there's a genre that really excites you, make sure you discuss that with the agent before you sign on the dotted line. You don't want to find out after the fact that they don't have contacts in the area you're looking to go after.

How do you know when you're ready to get an agent? That's a question with as many answers as voice talent. Generally, I'd say you shouldn't approach an agent until you are solidly trained and have a couple jobs under your belt, so you can at least say you're out there working.

There are far more voice actors than agents to represent them, and agencies are inundated with new talent requests all the time. They can pick and choose who to work with, and it helps if you have a track record. Normally agents will only be interested in someone new if they fill a hole in their talent pool. Maybe you sound like a teenager, and the agent's roster is light on young voices? You're more likely to get a listen than someone who doesn't have that vocal quality.

The process of getting an agent can be pretty straightforward. Do some research, find the agencies you'd like to work with, and follow their instructions on submitting. Some will have very detailed directions on their website. Others will only accept new talent if they come by industry referral. You have to do your homework and figure out which agents might be a good match for you.

How can you find that out? Start with agents in your home market. If you live in a large metro area, chances are there's a talent agent who reps voice actors. On the other hand, if you're nowhere near an agent, there are agencies who work mostly online and service clients all over the country.

Once you've decided where you want to put your effort (commercials, animation, audiobook narration, etc.), a simple online search can give you some names of voice talent who have the career that you're going after. A couple clicks on iSpot, IMDb, or Audible, and you should be able to find out which agents those talent are with. Now you have a bullseye to shoot for.

Some talent agents service clients mostly in their geographic area, while others pitch their talent nationwide and internationally. I'm originally from Chicago, which operates as the casting hub for a good part of the Midwest, yet talent represented by those agencies will also get to audition for work that's based on one of the coasts.

Larger talent agencies in NYC and LA tend to focus on placing talent in projects with ad agencies and production companies there, yet they also work with international clients looking for English speakers.

The internet has opened up casting to anyone and everyone. It's responsible for making the voice over industry so much more exciting and challenging than when it was a local industry.

Podcasts can provide good info on the business, agents included. Check out *All Over VO* with my buddy Kiff VandenHeuvel, *The Bee Hive* with Kay Bess, *Voice Over Body Shop* with George Whittam and Dan Lenard, and the Mike Lenz VO podcast.

One quick note: all legitimate talent agents will represent you for free and take commission only when a client hires you. They will not require an up-front payment to represent you or require you to take their classes or record a demo with them. If you come across an agent who does this, find someone else. They are likely more interested in your money than your VO skills.

Some legitimate talent agencies do charge talent a fee to post their demos on their websites. This is usually a one-time cost and helps pay for running the site. Agencies who charge talent in this way are not trying to rip you off. Chances are their site attracts way more producers looking to hire talent than your site, so it can't hurt to be included.

In short, agents can be a game changer for your career simply because they open so many doors that would otherwise be closed.

Things a Membership to a VO Site Can Do

If agents are the gatekeepers of the work, does that mean you can't audition for VO without one? Nope. You can go it alone by joining a voice over casting site.

Part of the gig economy, these sites allow clients to bypass traditional agents. Clients post auditions, algorithms send them to a selection of the site's members, and the talent read for the job. The client listens to the auditions, chooses a voice, and either the site or the client notifies the talent who booked it.

Sometimes the voice actor's fee is paid directly to them, and other times the fee goes through the website, which takes a cut before the talent sees any money. Sometimes the site demands both a membership fee and a cut of your earnings.

There are some pros and cons to using these sites. On the positive side, they allow anyone to have a shot at actual paying work. As long as you pay membership fees, you'll be in the running for jobs to which you wouldn't have had access prior to joining. Seems like a good way to get your feet wet, a huge advantage when you're just starting out.

But there is a downside. These sites are generally crammed with talent, and you are at the mercy of the algorithm. If it doesn't think you fit the job specs, you won't be sent the audition. Also, the voice actors who read an audition when it's first posted tend to book the most work. If you're a client and you want to hear thirty auditions, when you find what you need on number four, you're not going to listen to numbers five through thirty.

Speaking of clients, posting auditions is always free. As a result, many clients use these sites as backups in case they don't find what they need through agents. That means a lot of auditions are posted, read for, and ignored. You can chalk it up to getting some practice, but it's a real bummer to work hard on an audition that will never be heard.

Rounding out the list of cons, a couple of these sites have horrible reputations for keeping a large portion of fees voice actors make. Spend some time on the Voice Acting subreddit on Reddit.com. You'll figure out which sites are trusted by the VO community and which are considered giant rip-offs.

I am personally not a fan of membership sites. To me, it always feels like a game is being played with talent's money. For one thing, some operate as talent agencies with ridiculous commission rates, negotiating high fees for jobs and keeping far more than any real agent would keep for themselves. Others stay away from talent fees, but burden voice actors with annual membership costs in the hundreds of dollars. Still others collect both membership fees and commissions, which I think is particularly ridiculous.

More than one VO membership site has a membership costing thousands of dollars annually. Allegedly these members are guaranteed access to any and all auditions posted on the site. But I don't know... none of these sites operate transparently, so you never really know what you're getting or missing out on. You just have to trust that your fees are buying you the access you're promised. Of course, you then have to book enough work to cover the cost of that membership.

On the other hand, I can see how they might be tempting for someone trying to establish a VO business. They seem like an easy way to get started and build a client base, and that may be true. But I would approach them with caution, and I would certainly stay away from sites that keep a portion of your earnings.

A real talent agent will always keep 10 percent (if you're a member of a performance union) up to a maximum of 15 percent (if you're nonunion) of the fee from your work. That's how the real world works. It's up to you to decide whether or not it's worth paying membership sites to play the audition game.

STEP SEVEN: REPEAT

You know the difference between a job and a career. A job is something you do to make money. A career is a series of connected opportunities, each having an effect on your future in that industry. That means starting out doing a local radio spot and ending up being the live announcer on a major entertainment awards show years later, like a friend of mine.

A voice over job might bring you a couple hundred bucks, but a career can lead to so much more. These seven steps are a guide to building a career.

But this step, repeat, is possibly the most important because it will keep your career rolling. Voice over is not the kind of business you can set and forget. You can't take a class, do a job or two, and sit back and let it rain money. You'll have to revisit each of these steps so you can stay relevant and keep working.

Let's review them.

Step 1: Listen

Reads are always coming in and out of fashion, and you have to stay on trend. Celebrities exert a ton of influence over read styles, and the rest of us have to keep up and adapt.

For a while, Mike Rowe was in high demand. As host of the show *Dirty Jobs*, he had a masculine, everyman feel that brands really loved. Male VO talent saw a lot of auditions with specs that used him as a celebrity reference. Female talent are commonly asked to think of Rashida Jones, Tina Fey, or Scarlett Johansson as references.

In other words, talent have to do their best to emulate the delivery of celebrities. If that doesn't come naturally, they have to revisit...

Step 2: Train

It's always beneficial to have a knowledgeable second set of ears guiding you through new read styles.

When times change, talent have to change with them. When I got started, the term "announcer" meant a completely different thing than it does now. Back then, we were still in the era of authority. A deep-voiced guy would nearly command you to buy something. Today, any sense of sell in a read is usually undesirable unless we're talking about retail spots for car brands.

I worked with a coach long and hard to get that old "announcer" out of my reads. But let's say your commercial career is taking a bit of a dip. Time to adapt, again.

Step 3: Find Your Focus

To give yourself more chances to book work, you'll need to explore more corners of voice over.

Not everyone will do everything, but you can easily specialize in one or two areas. If you want an animation career, there's no reason you can't have one if you develop your voices and get them out there. Most of this work comes out of Los Angeles, so if you don't live in SoCal, YouTube and/or Twitter might be your best friend. You'll have to get creative to get the word out that you've got some killer characters living inside of you.

Or maybe you'd like some steady, longer-term work and are curious about audiobooks. Check out ACX.com and get yourself going there. The longer you stay in business, the more you'll want to upgrade your versatility.

Step 4: Invest In Gear

Just as you should always be looking to add to your VO tool belt, you should also be looking to periodically improve your gear.

If you've got a USB mic, look to upgrade to XLR. If you've got one of those, consider adding another one for different styles of auditions, or add software to clean up your audio.

Booths are always upgradable. I have a friend who built his own, and everything sounded great except for a hum that just wouldn't go away. It was low, but it was there, and he worked around it for a while before he finally isolated the source: a boiler in his condo building. Turns out the solution involved placing some rubber feet on the bottom of the booth, giving it some separation between the floor of his condo and the lower frame of his booth.

Unless you record in a professional recording studio, there's always room for improvement. Speaking of improving...

Step 5: Build Demos

You will always want to change up your demos. I don't care how experienced you get, the idea of updating your demos will always be on the table.

When you're beginning your career, you'll think your demos sound really great. Then you'll get a little better, and they'll seem...less so. Knowing that everyone from agents to potential clients are listening to them, you'll want to make sure they're always showcasing your very best work.

When you're experienced and feel your work slowing down, redoing your demos will be the first thing you'll think of. As you get more confident and comfortable with voice over, I'm willing to lighten up on my rules for demos. You can eventually work on your own.

As you book work, try to get copies of everything you do in case you can use part of the project in a demo. Do this enough and you may never again have to pay someone to help you build a demo.

Step 6: Market

Marketing is really about creating and maintaining relationships. Voice over is a relationship business as much as it's a creative one. You'll hopefully have lots of clients and producers to keep in touch with. You may have multiple agents. But you'll also be reaching out to the world, letting potential employers know that you're very good at what you do and available to do it.

Social media is a great way to do that. I'm not a great role model because my social media is pretty seriously lacking. But there are plenty of people who use social platforms to support their career efforts, and there's no reason why you can't as well. If you'd like to follow me and say hello, here are my handles:

Twitter: @ChrisAgos
Instagram: @ChrisAgos
YouTube: youtube.com/ChrisAgosActor

By the time you read this, we may have a Complete-Voiceover.com page on Facebook too.

Step 7: Repeat

By now you've learned that having a voice over career requires cultivation and dedication. But let me tell you, it's so worth it.

I have an active on-camera career that grew out of my VO work, but the thing that brings me the most income in the shortest amount of time is voice over. I love acting on camera, but there's a lot that goes into it. I have to get to auditions, worry about how I look, what I wear, and I have to memorize lines. Once I'm booked, the hours are long, and sometimes I have to go out of town for work, leaving my wife to handle everything at home.

I'm not complaining, I'm certainly not going to stop acting because of these things, but my voice over career is just so much simpler. I audition at home, I book stuff, I show up to a studio in jeans and a t-shirt, and I talk for an hour. Or I do the job from my booth.

And often, it's financially more lucrative than on-camera work. My best year was the result of having one VO client who was responsible for over 60 percent of my income. I have a friend who was the voice of a major chain of home improvement stores for a while. He said it wasn't so much an income change as it was a lifestyle change. He earned enough to buy a house, send a couple kids to grad school, and put some away for retirement. He didn't need the money, he was doing just fine without that client, but it catapulted his income into the stratosphere.

Can you imagine being in a career where you're just one job away from that kind of financial windfall? Welcome to the world of VO. By the way, those life-changing jobs are only available in the union world.

FINAL THOUGHTS

Consider yourself armed with enough information to get going in VO. I hope you feel more prepared than you did before reading this book.

Don't let your learning stop here. Visit Complete-Voiceover.com for more books that dive deep into specific corners of the industry like commercials, movie trailers, promos and more. All of our authors are working pros and we've come together to educate you, so take advantage of our expertise.

I want to leave you with one last story. My first voice over teacher said, "Remember that the longer you stay in this industry, the more of a veteran you'll be, even if you hardly ever work." It was his way of telling me that persistence would be the key to my career.

That's still true today. Do you have any idea how many people want to be voice talent? Loads. It's why there are so many schools, coaches, and online resources available.

If you don't believe me, just ask any agent. Their inboxes are filled with people looking for representation or just asking questions. A friend of mine spent a couple years as the receptionist at a talent agency. She said half the people who called just wanted some information on how to get started.

Know how many of those people didn't do anything beyond make that call? Again, I'd say loads. Getting into this business isn't easy, and it takes a combination of determination, strategy, and perseverance.

Many people who start auditioning will give up when they don't book something right away. Many who land representation will get discouraged when their agent doesn't send them as many auditions as they hoped.

When this happens to you, I hope you'll stay in the trenches. The longer you hang in there, the more familiar your name will become to those who can help you. At some point a door will open, and you'll be there to walk through it while many of your peers will have given up.

Even if you don't book a single thing, you'll be a veteran of the business by default.

If you're persistent and professional, you'll begin to work. As you do, don't be discouraged by dry spells. Everyone has them. It's part of being in this business.

As for me, I had plenty of opportunities to quit. Twenty years' worth of them, actually. Starting out wasn't easy back then, either. My goal was to work once a month, and when that happened, I upped that goal to twice a month, and so on.

There were plenty of months that I didn't work at all, and it would have been easy to give up. I guess I just wanted it too badly.

Sometimes it comes down to that. Do you want to be a voice talent? Then do it. People will tell you it won't happen. They'll say it's just too difficult. They mean well, but they're wrong because obviously it's very doable.

Keep training, auditioning, networking, and moving forward. Before long, you'll be the one helping others get started.

I hope you get everything you deserve out of this business. I wish you all the best!

BONUS: ACTIONABLE LIST

I gave you seven steps to start your career, but now that you have a good overview of the voice over industry, what can you do right this minute? Here's a list of actions you could take. All of them are free and will bring you one step closer to starting your career.

- Set three short-term (one to three months) achievable goals. Write them down and date the document.
- If you're feeling overwhelmed, tackle one thing at a time. It's a marathon, not a sprint.
- Get updated when we release new books, videos and other training resources by signing up for them at **https://www.complete-voiceover.com/signup**
- Spend ten minutes a day browsing commercials on iSpot.tv.
- Start a list of voices you like. Then start a list of voices you hear that are like yours.
- Acknowledge any fears about starting. Afraid of failing, not being the right age, or losing money? No one who played it safe ever made it big.
- Spend sixty minutes a week watching voice over content on recommended YouTube channels.

- Search for a VO studio or acting school in your area and read reviews.
- Look up some coaches. Read and listen to what they have to say.
- Visit a big-box music store and ask about microphones. Clerks sometimes really know what they're talking about.
- Resolve to listen to every commercial, all the way through.
- Look into joining a VO/VA Facebook group.
- Look around your house and figure out where you could put a booth.
- Make a list of things you see as barriers to starting. Think about how to get past them because problems have solutions.
- Look for a website template you could turn into www.yournameVO.com.
- Put together a start-up budget.
- Reach out to established voice talent and ask someone to mentor you.
- Subscribe to one or more VO podcasts.
- Download an audiobook. Listen to how the talent tells the story. Audible offers free trials.
- Search for talent agencies in your home town and read their requirements for new talent submissions.
- Start listening closely to commercials made by big brands. Compare them to the reads on smaller, lesser-known brands.
- Follow advertising trade publications on social media: *AdWeek*, *Advertising Age*, etc.
- Watch animated shows and see if you can identify how many voices an actor contributes to an episode.
- Watch a documentary and pay special attention to the narrator.
- Think about which parts of the business interest you the most. Audiobooks? Long-form narration?

GLOSSARY OF TERMS

Ad agency – A company hired by a brand to generate content that will benefit that brand.

Ad copy – The text of an advertisement, sometimes shortened to just "copy."

Agent – Someone who represents voice talent.

Audition – A tryout for a particular job.

Axis – The center point of a microphone.

Booking – A firm offer for work, a job.

Booth – An isolated and sound-treated area used for recording.

Copywriter – Someone who writes ad copy.

Creatives – People responsible for the look and feel of advertising content. Writers, designers, etc.

Demo – A sampling of a voice talent's abilities.

Mic – A microphone.

Phantom Power – A method of supplying electricity to a microphone that lacks a built-in power source.

Read – A delivered interpretation of a script or bit of ad copy.

Script – Written words to be read by voice actors on a particular job.

Session – A recording session, the act of recording a project.

Spot – A commercial meant for distribution on air or online.

Talent – A voice actor. Voiceover, voice talent, and voice actor are interchangeable terms.

ACKNOWLEDGMENTS

This book wouldn't have been possible without input from Ray Van Steen, Kurt Naebig, Robyn Moler, Bill Lloyd, Thomson Howell, Kiff VandenHeuval, and Nicola Santoro, and the hundreds of former students who taught me how to teach. I owe debts of gratitude to copy editor Elizabeth Owen and book designers/consultants Tim Pettingale and Joseph Alexander at self-published.co.uk. None of my writing, or any other work I do, would be possible without the love and support of my wife, Patricia and our two boys. I thank them with everything I have.

55571461R00056